A Kid's Guide to Drawing America™

How to Draw
Michigan's
Sights and Symbols

Jenny Deinard

The Rosen Publishing Group's
PowerKids Press™
New York

For Weston Quasha

Published in 2002 by The Rosen Publishing Group, Inc.
29 East 21st Street, New York, NY 10010

First Edition

Book Design: Kim Sonsky
Layout Design: Dean Galiano
Project Editors: Jannell Khu, Jennifer Landau

Illustration Credits: Jamie Grecco
Photo Credits: p. 7 © Index Stock; p. 8 (self-portrait and sketch), 9 (painting) © Grand Rapids Art Museum, Gift of George and Barbara Gordon, 1988.1.9; pp. 12, 14 © One Mile Up, Incorporated; p. 16 © Patrick Johns/CORBIS; p. 18 © Richard Hamilton Smith/CORBIS; p. 20 © Pam Gardner; Frank Lane Picture Agency/CORBIS; p. 22 © S.S. Milwaukee Clipper Preservation, Inc.; p. 24 © Bill Howes; Frank Lane Picture Agency/CORBIS; p. 26 © D. Robert Franz/CORBIS; p. 28 © Bettmann/CORBIS.

Deinard, Jenny
        How to draw Michigan's sights and symbols /
Jenny Deinard.
            p. cm. — (A kid's guide to drawing America)
        Includes index.
        Summary: This book explains how to draw some of Michigan's sights and symbols, including the state seal, the official flower, and the Milwaukee Clipper, the oldest U.S. passenger steamship on the Great Lakes.
        ISBN 0-8239-6078-1
        1. Emblems, State—Michigan—Juvenile literature 2. Michigan—In art—Juvenile literature
3. Drawing—Technique—Juvenile literature   [1. Emblems, State—Michigan   2. Michigan
3. Drawing—Technique]   I. Title   II. Series
        2001
        743'.8'99774—dc21

Manufactured in the United States of America

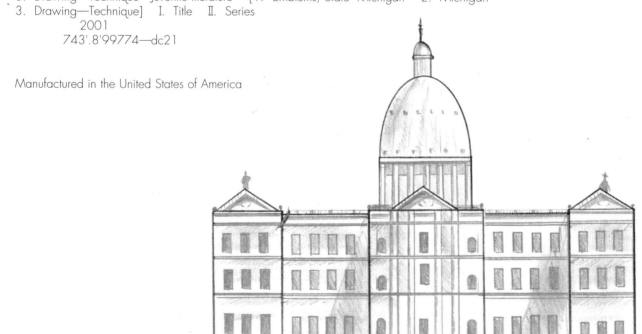

CONTENTS

Let's Draw Michigan

About 10,000 years ago, Native Americans began living in the area we now call Michigan. In 1668, a French explorer and Jesuit priest named Jacques Marquette built the first European settlement in Michigan. The French named the settlement Sault Sainte Marie. When the French and Indian War ended in 1763, the British took control of Michigan. Twenty years later, the British agreed to give up Michigan when they lost an area called the Northwest Territory in the American Revolution. It wasn't until 1796, however, that the British finally left. Michigan officially joined the United States as a state on January 26, 1837.

In 1896, businessman Henry Ford began making automobiles in Michigan. The city of Detroit and the entire state still play a big part in the motor vehicle industry. In fact Michigan is known as the automotive capital of the world, and Detroit, its largest city, is known as Motor City. Detroit also is home to Motown Records, one of the leaders in the music industry.

Other industries in Michigan include metal products,

chemicals, and tourism. Michigan ranks first in the agricultural production of red sour cherries, dry beans, and blueberries.

Michigan has many exciting sights and symbols. You will learn how to draw some of them with this book. A simple shape begins each drawing. From there you add other shapes. Under each drawing, directions explain how to do the step. New steps are shown in red. You can check out the drawing terms for help, too.

You will need the following supplies to draw Michigan's sights and symbols:

- A sketch pad
- An eraser
- A number 2 pencil
- A pencil sharpener

Here are some words and shapes you will need to draw Michigan's sights and symbols:

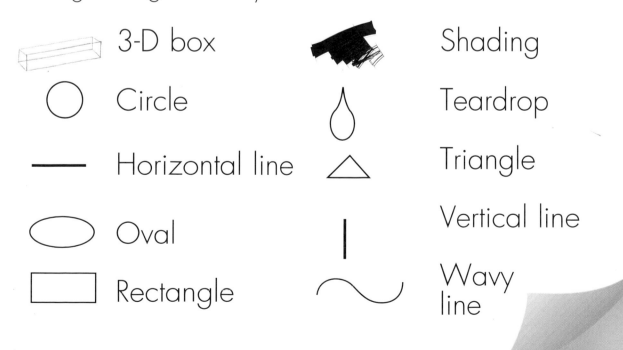

3-D box

Shading

Circle

Teardrop

Horizontal line

Triangle

Oval

Vertical line

Rectangle

Wavy line

The Great Lakes State

Michigan's official nickname is the Great Lakes State because it borders on four of the five Great Lakes. These bordering lakes are Michigan, Erie, Huron, and Superior. In fact no matter where you are in Michigan, you are only 85 miles (137 km) away from one of four Great Lakes. Forty of Michigan's 83 counties border on one of the Great Lakes. Michigan also has 11,000 inland lakes and 36,000 miles (57,936 km) of streams. Michigan covers a total area of 96,705 square miles (250,465 sq km) and has a population of 9,863,800. Michigan also is called the Wolverine State because early fur trappers traded wolverine pelts for money. The state's name means "great lake" and comes from the Native American word *michigama*. There are 125,700 people who live in Lansing, the state capital. The most populated city is Detroit, which has more than a million residents.

This picture shows a sunset on Lake Michigan, near the city of South Haven.

Artist in Michigan

Mathias Alten was born in Gusenburg, Germany, in 1871. While in Germany, Alten apprenticed under an artist named Joseph Klein and learned how to paint ceiling and wall decorations. At the

Artist Mathias Alten

age of 17, he and his family moved to Grand Rapids, Michigan. In America Alten earned his reputation as a skilled painter and decorator. He first exhibited his work in 1896, at the Michigan State Fair. In 1898, he moved back to Europe to study art in a more formal setting. After living in an artists' colony in Étaples, on the northern coast of France near Boulogne and painting fishing

Mathias Alten created this sketch for a landscape painting. For this sketch, he used graphite on paper.

scenes, he moved to Paris. He studied at the Académie Julian and then traveled throughout Europe. Alten was an accomplished painter of landscapes, portraits, flowers, and animals. His work was unusual for his time, because he focused on working-class people, often showing them in rural scenes. Alten returned to Grand Rapids in the early 1900s and had exhibits in the city every year. He liked to paint the Grand River in Grand Rapids as well as Reeds Lake, which was near his home. Alten went back to Europe to paint for a year, and, after a brief return to America, went back again in 1912. Alten died in Europe on March 8, 1938, but he remains one of Michigan's most respected artists.

Alten painted *Picnic at Macatawa* in 1940. The scene of this Michigan city was painted in oil on canvas and measures 40" x 30" (102 cm x 76 cm).

Map of Michigan

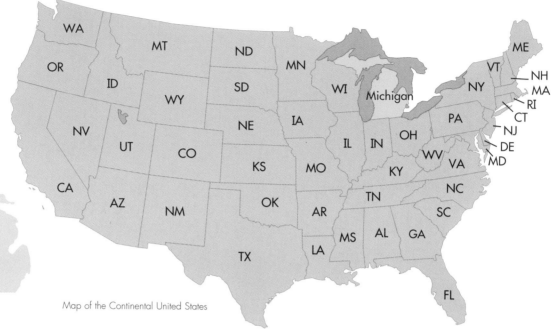

Map of the Continental United States

Michigan is broken up into two parts, the Upper Peninsula and the Lower Peninsula. Lake Michigan separates these areas. Not as many people live on the Upper Peninsula as on the Lower Peninsula. In fact 90 percent of the Upper Peninsula is forest. Michigan has 3,288 miles (5,291.5 km) of shoreline, more than any other state, except Alaska. The highest point in Michigan is Mt. Arvon, which stands 1,979 feet (603 m) above sea level. Mt. Arvon is located northwest of Marquette in the Huron Mountains of the Upper Peninsula. Michigan borders Ohio, Indiana, and the country of Canada. Michigan's three national forests are Ottawa, Hiawatha, and Huron-Manistee.

1

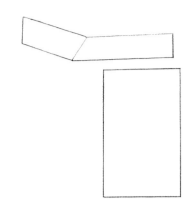

Start by drawing a vertical rectangle. Draw two shapes that connect at an angle above the rectangle.

2

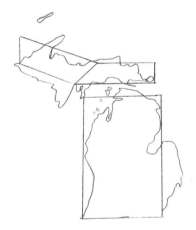

Using the shapes and rectangle as a guide, draw the outline of Michigan.

3

Erase extra lines and draw an X to mark Sleeping Bear Dunes National Lakeshore. Draw a square to mark St. Ignace Mission.

4

Draw a circle to mark the city of Detroit, and a triangle to mark Ottawa National Forest.

5

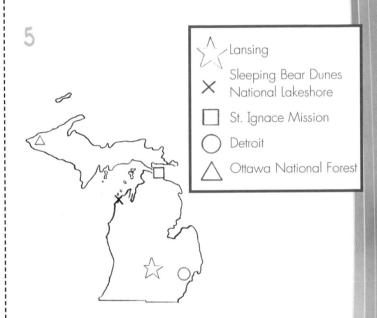

☆ Lansing

✕ Sleeping Bear Dunes National Lakeshore

☐ St. Ignace Mission

◯ Detroit

△ Ottawa National Forest

To finish your map, draw a star to mark Lansing, the capital of Michigan.

The State Seal

Michigan's state seal was designed by Lewis Cass, the state's first governor, in 1835, and it was adopted that year. In the center of the seal rests a shield surrounded by an elk and a moose, two animals native to Michigan. On the shield is a man waving his right hand and holding a gun in his left hand. This represents peace and the man's ability to defend his rights. The man stands on a peninsula next to water. On his left is a rising sun, which signifies hope and the promise of a bright future. Above the shield stands an eagle, a national symbol of the United States. The eagle holds an olive branch, a symbol of peace. The 13 fruits on the branch stand for America's first 13 colonies. Michigan's motto, If You Seek A Pleasant Peninsula, Look About You, is written in Latin on a banner beneath the eagle's feet.

1

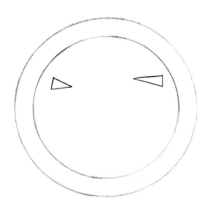

Draw two circles, one inside the other. Add two triangles for the elk's and the moose's heads.

2

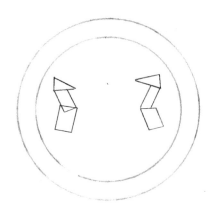

Add four rectangles for the bodies of the elk and the moose.

3

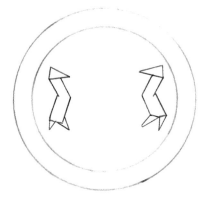

Erase extra lines. Add four triangles for the elk's and the moose's legs.

4

Finish the legs with thin rectangles. Draw the shapes of the elk and the moose.

5

Erase extra lines. Draw the eyes and the antlers on the elk and the moose. Add a tail to the elk.

6

Add the words "THE GREAT SEAL OF THE STATE OF MICHIGAN" on top and the letters and Roman numerals "A.D.MDCCCXXXV." at the bottom. Add detail and shading. To learn how to draw the center of the seal, look at the Michigan state flag instructions.

13

The State Flag

The state flag of Michigan was accepted in 1911, and it is the image of the state's coat of arms on a blue background. The coat of arms is the same image that is on the state seal. In 1972, Harold G. Coburn wrote a pledge of allegiance that pays tribute to Michigan's flag. The words of the pledge are, "I pledge allegiance to the flag of Michigan, and to the state for which it stands, two beautiful peninsulas united by a bridge of steel, where equal opportunity and justice to all is our ideal." The bridge to which the pledge refers is the Mackinac Bridge, a 5-mile (8-km) bridge that runs over the Straits of Mackinac and that connects the upper and lower peninsulas of Michigan.

1

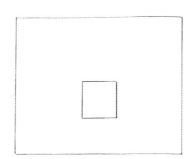

Start by drawing a large rectangle for the flag's field. Add a small rectangle in the center for the shield.

2

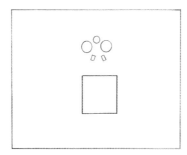

Add three circles for the eagle's wings and its head. Draw two small rectangles for its legs.

3

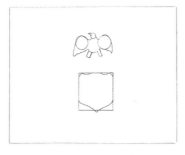

Draw in the shape of the eagle. Draw the outline of the shield.

4

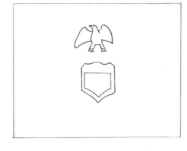

Erase extra lines. Add the eagle's feet and the center of the shield.

5

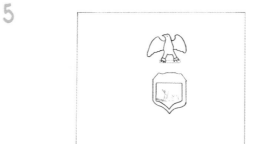

Add a rectangle between the eagle's feet. Draw detail in the center of the shield.

6

Add detail to the eagle and the shield. To learn how to draw the elk and the moose, refer to the Michigan state seal instructions.

The Apple Blossom

The apple blossom (*Pyrus coronaria*) is native to Michigan and became the official state flower in 1897. The apple trees on which the blossoms grow are an important part of the state's economy. Michigan is the second-largest apple producer in the country. The state has more than 58,000 acres (23,472 ha) of apple orchards and produces more than a billion pounds (373 billion kg) of apples every year. A woman named Anna Eliza Woodcock helped to choose the state flower. In 1897, she rolled a wheelbarrow full of apple blossoms two blocks from her own apple tree to the capitol building. She did this to prove that the state should choose the fragrant flower to be the state's official flower.

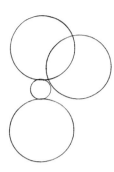

Start by drawing a circle for the center of the flower. Add three circles around the center for the petals.

2

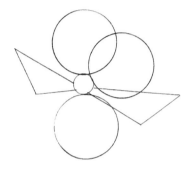

Add two triangles to finish the basic shape of the flower's petals.

3

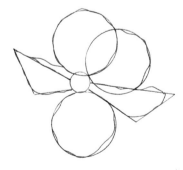

Start drawing in your petals using the circles and triangles as guides.

4

Erase extra lines. Add four small triangles in the center. Add other details as shown.

5

Add short, straight lines with circles at the ends to finish the flower's center. Erase extra lines.

6

Add shading and detail to your flower and you're done. You also can add a stem.

The White Pine

The white pine (*Pinus strobus*) became the official tree of Michigan in 1955. From 1870 to the early 1900s, Michigan was the number-one lumber producer in the United States. The white pine also is known as the eastern white pine, the spruce pine, and the northern white pine. It grows in the northeastern United States, where it is a native tree. The bark of the white pine is a purplish gray, and it has deep ridges. The leaves, or needles, range from bluish green to silver-green and are about 2½ to 5 inches (6–13 cm) long. The leaves grow in a bundle, or cluster, of five.

1

Start by drawing a long, thin triangle for the tree trunk.

2

To draw the shape of the tree, add a larger triangle on top of the thin triangle.

3

Draw branches by adding curvy lines from the tree trunk to the edge of the larger triangle.

4

Once you've finished your branches, erase the large triangle.

5

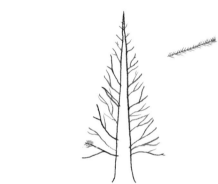

Draw short, straight lines on each branch to create the tree's needles. If you need help, look at the close-up of the needles. You can add more branches to make the tree look fuller.

6

Shade in the branches and the tree trunk, and the tree is complete.

19

The Robin

The robin (*Turdus migratorius*) belongs to a group of birds called thrushes. The bird got its name from English colonists who thought it looked like a bird in England called a robin redbreast. This bird became Michigan's state bird in 1931. Male robins are mostly a brownish gray color with a red underbelly. The female robin has no red breast and is a duller color of the same brownish gray. Robins are about 8–9 inches (20–23 cm) long with a 4-inch-long (10-cm-long) tail. Robins stay clear of people. They have strong, musical voices. Female robins lay three or four blue eggs. Once the eggs hatch, the male robin cares for the brood while the female prepares for another brood. Robins eat beetles, caterpillars, spiders, earthworms, and snails.

1

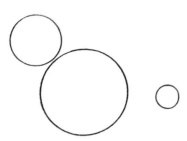

Draw three circles for the robin's outer shape.

2

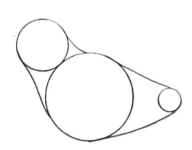

Connect your circles to form the shape of the bird's body.

3

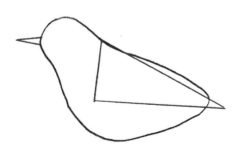

Erase extra lines. Add two triangles, one for the beak and one for the wing.

4

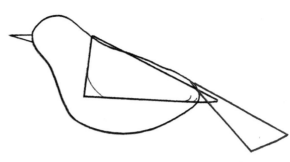

Add a triangle for the tail. Round off the bird's wing.

5

Erase extra lines. Draw in the eye, the legs, the feet, and the shape of the wing. Add detail to the end of the tail.

6

Add shading and detail to your bird, and you're done.

The SS *Milwaukee Clipper*

The SS *Milwaukee Clipper* is the oldest U.S. passenger steamship on the Great Lakes. Called the SS *Juniata* when it was first built in 1904, the ship measures 361 feet by 45 feet (110 m x 14 m). The Pennsylvania Railroad used the *Juniata* to carry passengers and freight until 1915, when it became illegal for railroad companies to own steamships. The ship was owned by the Great Lakes Transit Corporation and then by the Manitowoc Shipbuilding Company. It was this company that renamed the ship the *Milwaukee Clipper*. The ship stopped carrying passengers in 1970. It is now a floating maritime history learning center in Muskegon, Michigan.

1

To make the hull, or body, of the ship, draw a squared-off triangle. There should be a notch in the triangle as shown.

2

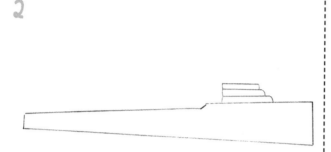

Add three rectangles with rounded edges on top of the hull.

3

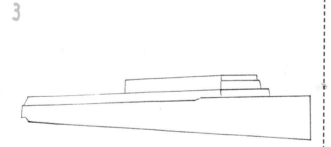

Draw two more long rectangles.

4

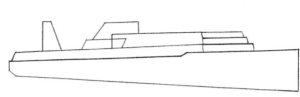

Draw three four-sided shapes as shown.

5

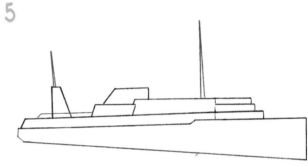

Add a thin rectangle at the rear of the ship. Draw two thin triangles as shown.

6

Use small rectangles for windows and doors. Add shading and detail to your ship and you're done. You also can add water and a flag for extra detail.

The Brook Trout

The brook trout (*Salvelinus fontinalis*) is native to Michigan and was chosen as the state fish in 1988. Brook trout are usually from 10 to 12 inches (25–30 cm) long, but some can be as long as 21 inches (53 cm). Most brook trout weigh from 4 to 6 pounds (2–3 kg), but the largest one ever caught weighed 14.5 pounds (6.5 kg)!

Brook trout are found in streams and lakes all around North America. They are known by other names, too, including brookie, char, speckled trout, and mud trout. Brook trout have backs that range in color from olive green to dark brown with silvery sides and pale spots.

1

Start by drawing a long rectangle for the fish's body.

2

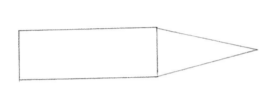

Add a triangle to the rectangle to finish the shape of the body.

3

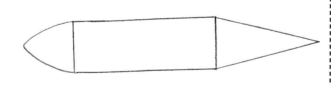

Draw the fish's head using a curved shape as shown.

4

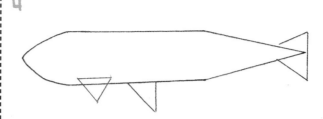

Erase any extra lines, and add three triangles for the fish's tail and its fins.

5

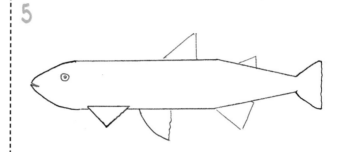

Erase extra lines, and add three more triangles, an eye and a mouth. Round off the bottom middle fin.

6

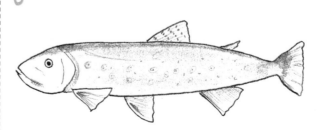

Add detail and shading, and your fish is done.

The White-Tailed Deer

Michigan adopted the white-tailed deer (*Odocoileus virginianus*) as its official animal in 1997. White-tailed deer are 3–3½ feet (1–1¼ m) tall and weigh 100–350 pounds (45–159 kg). Their fur is gray in the winter and turns reddish in the summer. Female deer don't have antlers. The antlers of the male deer, or bucks, begin to grow in the spring. In the fall the skin, or velvet, on their antlers starts to fall off. If you see a buck scratching his antler, it's because the velvet itches when it begins to come off. White-tailed deer eat leaves, grass, bark, acorns, and apples. Female deer give birth to one or two deer at a time. Fawns, or baby deer, have white spots when they are born.

1

Start by drawing two circles and a triangle for the deer's body and head.

2

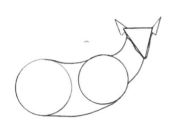

Connect the triangle and circles to form the deer. Add two small triangles for ears.

3

Erase extra lines. Draw four slanted rectangles for the tops of the deer's legs.

4

Draw four thin rectangles to finish the legs and four small squares for hooves. Add the deer's tail.

5

Finish the legs and add the eyes, a nose, and the antlers. Then erase extra lines and smudges.

6

Add shading and detail to your deer, and you're done.

Michigan's Capitol

Architect Elijah E. Myers, one of the country's most well known, post–Civil War builders of capitol buildings, designed the Michigan state capitol. The Michigan state capitol was completed in 1879, and it is located in Lansing, the state capital. The building is 420 feet (128 m) long, 274 feet (83.5 m) wide, and 267 feet (81 m) tall (including the spire). After the building was completed, artisans painted much of the interior walls using detailed patterns. The interior remains one of the best examples of Victorian painted decorative arts in this country. In 1992, the Michigan state capitol was placed on the list of National Historic Landmarks.

1

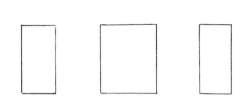

Start by drawing three rectangles for the wings of the capitol building.

2

Add three triangles.

3

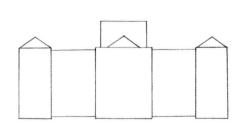

Draw three more rectangles to finish the shape of the building and the base of the dome.

4

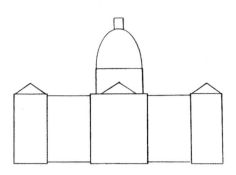

Draw a half oval and a rectangle for the dome.

5

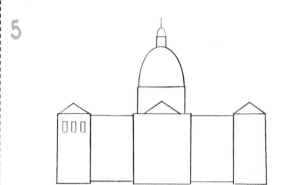

Add another half oval and a short, straight line for the top of the dome. You also can use rectangles to start the windows.

6

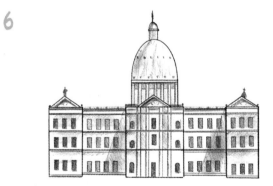

Add shading and detail to your building, and you're done. You also can use thin rectangles to add columns.

Michigan State Facts

Statehood	January 26, 1837, 26th state
Area	96,705 square miles (250,465 sq km)
Population	9,863,800
Capital	Lansing, population, 125,700
Most Populated City	Detroit, population, 1,012,100
Industries	Automobiles, machinery, metal products, office furniture, chemicals, and tourism
Agriculture	Cattle, vegetables, soybeans, corn, and hogs
Animal	White-tailed deer
Bird	Robin
Flower	Apple blossom
Wildflower	Dwarf lake iris
Fish	Brook trout
Tree	White pine
Gemstone	Greenstone
Stone	Petoskey stone
Soil	Kaklaska soil series
Motto	If You Seek A Pleasant Peninsula, Look About You
Reptile	Painted turtle
Nicknames	The Great Lakes State and the Wolverine State

Glossary

accomplished (uh-KOM-plisht) To have finished something well.

allegiance (uh-LEE-jents) Support of a country, group, or cause.

American Revolution (uh-MER-uh-ken reh-vuh-LOO-shun) Battles that soldiers from the colonies fought against England for freedom.

apprenticed (ah-PREN-tist) To have worked for a skilled person in order to learn a trade or an art.

architect (AR-kih-tekt) Someone who designs buildings.

brood (BROOD) Young birds hatched from eggs at the same time.

Civil War (SIH-vul WOR) The war fought between the northern and southern states of America from 1861 to 1865.

coat of arms (KOHT UV ARMZ) A design on or around a shield or on a drawing of a shield.

decorative (DEH-kuh-ruh-tihv) Having to do with an object or a design that makes something prettier.

fragrant (FRAY-grint) Something that smells.

French and Indian War (FRENCH AND IN-dee-in WOR)) A war fought between England and France over North American land, from 1756 to 1763.

industry (IN-dus-tree) A system of work, or labor.

Jesuit (JEH-zhoo-it) A member of a Roman Catholic society founded in 1534.

landmarks (LAND-marks) Important buildings, structures, or places.

maritime (MAR-ih-tym) Having to do with the sea, ships, or sea travel.

peninsula (peh-NIN-suh-luh) A piece of land that sticks out into water from a larger body of land.

Roman numerals (ROH-muhn NOOM-ruhlz) The letters that represent the numbers in the numbering system used by the ancient Romans.

spire (SPYR) A tall, narrow structure that comes to a point at the top.

Victorian (vik-TOR-ee-an) Having to do with the time when Queen Victoria ruled England.

Index

Web Sites

To learn more about Michigan, check out this Web site:
www.state.mi.us